CHANGES IN THE MATING STRATEGIES OF WHITE PEOPLE

Solange Castro

BROADWAY PLAY PUBLISHING INC
New York
www.broadwayplaypublishing.com
info@broadwayplaypublishing.com

CHANGES IN THE MATING STRATEGIES OF
WHITE PEOPLE
© Copyright 2019 Solange Castro

Cover art by Lilly Sur

First edition: July 2019
I S B N: 978-0-88145-851-0

Book design: Marie Donovan
Page make-up: Adobe InDesign
Typeface: Palatino

CHANGES IN THE MATING STRATEGIES OF WHITE PEOPLE premiered on 17 January 2014 at Lounge 2 Theater in Hollywood and ran until 23 February. The cast and creative contributors were:

JADE ....Abigail Marlowe
JOHN ....William Nicol
LOUISE ....Gloria Charles
TYLER...Kim Estes
DIRK...Brian Cousins
ROXANNE ....Sarah Underwood Saviano

Director...Craig Anton
Set design...Amanda Knehans
Lighting design ....Paige Stanley
Sound design.. Peter Carlstedt
Production stage manager ....Laure Jamme
Production consultant ....Leigh Fortier

THANK YOU

I wrote and produced this play independent of an established theater company. So up until the play's production, in 2014, most everyone I came into contact with contributed some form of support; financial, moral, spiritual, or a simple, "can't wait to see it."

Thank you, as always, to my late mother who supported every single word I wrote and weird creative thing I attempted. And thank you to my father, and family in general, for teaching me the value of being funny in this insane world.

Immense thanks to all who gave me general support, attended and/or acted in the many readings held in my tiny apartment, as well as the two staged readings, produced by Sylvia Loehndorf and Playwrights 6. These friends and professionals include Veronica Abney, Eileen Cabiling, Cody Chappel, Constance Haft, Jennifer Jameson, Alex Karlin, Ruth Katz, Danielle Kennedy, Joe Keyes, Darlene Levin, Donald Lopez, Todd Lowe, Monica Seggos, Michael Spellman, Sharlene Sullivan, Chloe Taylor, Rene Veillux, Greg Wolf, and Joan Wrzala.

This play could not have found publication without a production. Thanks to the generous donation of Kickstarter angels I was able to stage a six-week run. These angels include: Ryan Alford, Dong Sung An, Christopher Angel, Gabriella Valli Avina, Franz

Baldassini, Maria Bamford, Marilyn Bamford, Joel
Bamford, Jade Barclay, Aaron Baumhackl, Judy
Belcher, Nina Belcher, Marjorie Berger, Cicely
Bingener, Mark Bingener, Teri Bond, Allison Breen,
El Rey Brian, Mollie Brown, James Bruce, Jack Burns,
Janetta Burt, W Bruce Cameron, Erlinda G Castro,
Rafaela Castro, Jennifer Cohen, Tim Davis, Cliff
Dawes, Leila Decker, Raj Desai, Marya Dosti, Dana
Eagle, Veronica Eguiguren, Jim Erwin, Will Fey, Sarah
Fey, Daniel Frank, Mark Fujiwara, Robb Fulcher,
John Gamboa, Laura Gamboa, Anne Garcia-Romero,
Galen Gilbert, Allen Gittelson, Elsa Guerra, Jhony
Gutierrez, Tania Haladner, Sara Halpert, Christopher
Hecht, Marty Herman, Steve Hernandez, Edwin Hill,
Darlene Hodgetts, Eliana Horeczko, Sharon Houston,
Clinton Howard, Marcus Howard, Kira Hubbard,
Jennifer Jameson, Amy Johnson, Ruth Katz, Joe Keyes,
Erin Khue Ninh, Brian Kiley, Karl Wm Klein, Paul
Lair, Tanya Lauer, Carol Ann Leif, Errol Ivan Lewis,
Gerald Lewis, Sylvia Loehndorf, Rebecca Long, Donald
Roman Lopez, Linda Luevano, Michelle Machrone,
Raul Macias, Jorge Martin, Suzanne Masterson,
Emily McDowell, Michelle Pan Mendez, Amy Mew,
Cathryn Michon, Emily Miller, Russell Mills, Pauline
Mu, Maria Murakawa, Brian Ng, Anne Nguyen,
Danielle Ozymandias, Rabuko Pavia, Claudia Perez,
Jared Planas, Carole Raimondi, Louis Reyes, Kate
Rhoades, David Rosenfeld, Solomon Russell, Susannah
Schulman, Lori Seamon, Sarah Bamford Seidelmann,
Lorenzo Semple, Judith Shelton, Edward W Shorter,
Topher Smith, Andrew Solmssen, Kendall Sor, Ratana
Therakulsathit, Goro Toshima, Jennifer Vally, Maureen
Vaughan, Eric Damon Walters, Jeanine Ward, Jeffrey
C Weiss, James Woster, Gregg Yearwood, and Camilla
Zamboni.

Without a fantastic production, I would have never heard the encouragement of audience members who, years later, requested that I remount it or submit it for publication. Great thanks to Craig Anton for your tireless vision; the cast of gifted actors—Kim, Abigail, Brian, Sarah, Gloria, and Will; Amanda Knehans, Paige Stanley, and Peter Carlstedt for bringing the sound, look and feel of a coffee shop to life; Laure Jamme for your passionate stage management; Leigh Fortier for guiding me in the ways of LA theater production; my cousin Phil Hernandez and his pal Ernie Lewis for creating the groovy Latin-vibe Kickstarter video soundtrack; Jim Coughlin for patiently shooting the Kickstarter videos; Jared Planas for help with the website; and Lilly Sur for creating the perfect artwork.

And, finally, thank you to that mysterious energy that creates ideas and causes them to flow through my mind and into my computer.

NOTE ON MUSIC

For performance of copyrighted songs, arrangements
or recordings referenced in this play, permission
of the copyright owner(s) must be obtained. Other
songs, arrangements or recordings may be substituted
provided permission from the copyright owner(s) of
such songs, arrangements or recordings is obtained
or songs, arrangements or recordings in the public
domain may be substituted.

CHARACTERS & SETTING

JADE, *female, mid-30s, White, cerebral, single workaholic digital designer*

JOHN, *male, mid-30s, White, advertising creative director*

LOUISE, *female, late-50s to early 60s, African American, former house-wife studying to get her PhD*

TYLER, *male, early-60s, African-American, businessman and father*

DIRK, *male, mid-40s, White, owner of ad agency and shark*

ROXANNE, *female, early-50s, White, therapist*

Hip chain coffee shop in Los Angeles. 2014.

Scene 1

(*Coffee Shop Land. The deafening sound of a grinder, light conversation, the sounds of something like George Gershwin's S'Wonderful plays. From the sounds, it's evident that there are other people in the coffee shop. However, two women sit at tables facing the audience.*)

(*Decor: Halloween decorations*)

(LOUISE, *[late-50s to early-60s, African-American woman] sits alone typing away at her computer. She's wearing a moo-moo type of dress.*)

(*At the next table sits* JADE, *[late-30s, White woman] by herself, sporadically glancing at her phone. She wears a yoga outfit. She stretches, cracks her back, drinks some coffee.*)

(JOHN, *[mid-30s, White man] enters and looks around furtively. He is dressed in a T-shirt and jeans, but the Right Kind Of T-shirt and Jeans. He wears flip flops. He looks like he works somewhere where such an outfit would be considered suitable.*)

JOHN: Janice74?

JADE: Gonzo73?…

(JADE *takes a deep breathe and shakes his hand with the energy and physical intimacy reminiscent of a talk show host. She looks at* JOHN *with a frozen concentration.*)

JADE: …three, four, five. (*Takes a deep breathe*) Done. I hope I didn't weird you out.

JOHN: Uh…what were you doing?

JADE: *(Spoken as a run on sentence, babbling, yet serious)*
Did you know that you can tell everything about a
person within the first five seconds of meeting them?
…Human beings are actually incredibly instinctual
animals, with powerful psychic senses but they've been
dulled by our dependence on technology, fast food,
crappy shows…but if we get very still…they return.

JOHN: So, now you know everything about me?

JADE: *(She's still babbling.)* Well, that was thirty
seconds ago…it depends on what I manage to retain
from that moment, and then actually, choose to
trust and believe…there are so many layers of social
conditioning that I have to fight through to find my
true, honest to God, gut feeling. Personally. I don't
think you know anything about a person until…you've
smelled him.

(Dead silence ensues. JOHN appears shell shocked.)

JOHN: I usually go by the picture.

(More silence)

*(Lights go down on JADE and JOHN. Meanwhile, TYLER,
[early 60s, African-American man] walks towards LOUISE.
She stands up and then they both sit down.)*

(Lights go up on TYLER and LOUISE.)

*(TYLER starts to cry. First it's a whimper, but soon it
becomes noticeably loud.)*

TYLER: I can't believe you would throw away thirty
years of marriage!

LOUISE: Tyler. You asked me for a divorce…

TYLER: And you're going to give it to me? Just like that?

LOUISE: Tyler, you're a grown man. I assume you ask
for what you want.

TYLER: Then you really don't know me at all.

(Cut back to JADE *and* JOHN. *They continue to sit in dead silence.)*

JADE: I talk too much.

JOHN: *(Struggling)* Have you been on a lot of these things?

JADE: No. This is my first Coffee Date. Most of the guys who contact me write such inspirations as, "Hi!" Or "Whatcha doin' RIGHT NOW?" I have friends who've met guys, but the only guys that contact me work hard, play hard, and hang out in infinity pools...I think something in me attracts a working class ethos... it's like, no matter how much I read, or evolve, or go to therapy, I am fundamentally the daughter of a mechanic.

(More dead silence)

JADE: If you hadn't been named Gonzo I would never have opened the message.

JOHN: That's the idea.

JADE: What's the idea?

JOHN: To get a woman's attention. Cast a wide net.

JADE: Wide net...I never do that.

JOHN: So, what do you do?

JADE: Carry scissors with me.

JOHN: Ha.

JADE: Actually, I don't date much. Never. Honestly, I don't even want to be here right now.

JOHN: Oh... Okay.

JADE: It's really the beginning of the end, if you ask me.

JOHN: The end of what?

JADE: Relationships. Especially, long-term committed ones. They're becoming a thing of the past, like manual transmission and independent book stores... We're going back to becoming a tribal society. It used to be that the serial monogamists were the ones you had to look out for... Now, everyone is a serial monogamist, that's the norm, but the sex addicted guys are the ones that you have to spot. It's all speeding up...like global warming, and mobile platforms, but on the level of human relationships. The dismantling of an institution, no, really a mentality, that we exist as units of two, plus, whatever comes out of our vaginas... ours meaning, people who have one...like me. I mean, women... So, what kind of television shows do you like?

JOHN: Uh...you know, Janice. I just remembered that I left my oven on. *(Pause)* No, sorry...honestly, I just don't think this is the right thing for me. I'm sorry. Thanks for taking the time to meet me.

JADE: Jade. My name is Jade.

JOHN: Sorry. Jade... *(He gets up and extends his hand.)* Good luck, Jade.

JADE: You too, Gonzo.

JOHN: John.

(JOHN walks out. JADE sits alone. She looks up at her watch then puts her hands in her pocket and pulls out a wallet and some keys. She places them on the table.)

(Lights up on TYLER and LOUISE)

TYLER: What?

LOUISE: Your muffin.

TYLER: How is WHAT?

LOUISE: I said "How is your muffin?

TYLER: Oh. I thought you asked, "How was work today?"

LOUISE: That's not even the same number of syllables.

TYLER: Yes, it is. How. Was. Work. To. Day. How. Is. Your. Muff. In. Five syllables.

(Lights go down on TYLER and LOUISE. They go up on JOHN and JADE.)

(JOHN comes running back on stage in a panic.)

JOHN: Oh, thank God! ...I swear I'd kept these in my pocket. Did you see me pull anything out?

JADE: God, no. Please!

JOHN: Seriously, why didn't you tell me that I had left my wallet and keys here?

JADE: You were too busy running out the door...

JOHN: You could have come after me. You knew I'd be back.

JADE: Well, you can't start your car without your keys. I can if it's not the fancy ignition kind. But that's only because my dad was a mechanic.

JOHN: How did I not see them?

JADE: I lifted them.

JOHN: You, what?

JADE: When you walked in...I pick pocketed your jeans, it's an old trick I learned from my Uncle Pete... he was in the mafia.

JOHN: You pick pocketed me?! Why would you do that?

JADE: Habit, I guess. That's how I kept my ex from ever leaving for good. I always managed to take something important, car keys, credit cards, iPhone. Finally, one day, I didn't take anything...never saw him again.

JOHN: That's crazy!

JADE: Any crazier than running out the door like I'm some kind of axe murderer?

JOHN: That's no way to start a relationship with a total stranger. You need therapy.

JADE: I just wanted to make sure that something got started. Most men run before "Hello."

JOHN: Maybe men run from you because you scare them away.

JADE: Or, maybe, they make it easy for me to lift their wallets because they want to come back.

(JOHN *opens his wallet and looks at his money.*)

JADE: I don't need your money.

JOHN: That's what my ex said.

JADE: And, by the way, I have a therapist.

JOHN: This is what my brother warned me about... (*He counts his money and puts his wallet and keys back in, and starts to walk out the door.*)

JADE: (*Pause*) Look, I'm sorry about your wallet. You're right, that was juvenile. But, really, what are my options? Take your wallet or jump into bed with you within the hour. Am I wrong?

JOHN: Yes. A little. It's not the worst idea... Look, Janice...

JADE: Jade.

JOHN: Jade. What are you looking for?

JADE: I don't know...human connection. What are you looking for?

JOHN: Sex. Of course.

(JADE's *phone rings.*)

JOHN: Do you need to get that?

JADE: It was scheduled to ring so I could fake an emergency.

JOHN: I guess we're past the point of faking anything.

JADE: Then why are you still standing here?

JOHN: Maybe that thing you said about me running out the door. It's true.

JADE: Look, John. I just met you. I don't know anything about you. You think I'm weird. Maybe I am. Don't listen to me.

JOHN: Yes, but you took five seconds to get a primal first impression of me. What did you see?

JADE: Well, that was ten whole minutes ago. Everything is different now. Since then I betrayed your trust by stealing your wallet and you abandoned our coffee date…

JOHN: But ten minutes ago? Before all this happened, what did you see?

JADE: Well, if I can trust my gut instincts, I thought here's a guy who doesn't really want to get close to one woman because he thinks they're all crazy.

JOHN: That's absolutely one hundred percent accurate. I flee. I'm a fleer. I run for the hills.

JADE: I'm going to get a latte, do you need anything? It's on me.

JOHN: I'm missing a twenty.

JADE: Like I said…it's on me.

(JOHN *sits down.*)

(*Lights go down on* JADE *and* JOHN. *Lights go up on* LOUISE *and* TYLER.)

TYLER: Look, I have a disease.

LOUISE: I know. I wish codependency was as much fun.

TYLER: It was that damn therapist.

LOUISE: Roxanne has nothing to do with it. She supported my process.

TYLER: Wish I'd gotten the invite to the process party.

LOUISE: You had other priorities.

TYLER: Sarcasm.

LOUISE: I'm sorry.

TYLER: No, I like it. Expressed anger. Punitive. That's what we were missing.

LOUISE: You want abuse.

TYLER: Abuse. That's a strong word. Healthy anger. Remember James from work? His wife. She did the whole deal. Threw all his clothes and shit on the lawn. Kicked his ass out. He slept on the lawn and got pneumonia.

LOUISE: Not my style.

TYLER: But James and his wife (whose name I can't for the life of me remember) they're still together. Not your style, though.

LOUISE: Look, it doesn't matter anymore. It's not about the other…women. We've just gone our separate ways.

TYLER: I know. Your process.

(JOHN *pulls out his phone.*)

JADE: So, you were obsessed with her…

JOHN: No. I loved her. I thought she was "The One." I know the difference between love and obsession.

JADE: You know what you are?

JOHN: What?

JADE: A dude.

JOHN: Last I checked.

JADE: Dudes think there is this one woman out there…
if only… (insert bullshit story here). You're content to
have sex with every woman so long as this idealized
woman exists who could inspire fidelity…. And, yet,
that idea is what keeps you from committing to any
one woman…including The One!

JOHN: We didn't want the same things. Just because it
didn't work out doesn't mean that it wasn't love.

JADE: That ending worked great in Casablanca, but that
was 1942…when everybody not only got married, but
stayed married. It's 2014…we need a new ending.

JOHN: What's your ending?

(JADE's phone alarm rings.)

JOHN: Another emergency?

JADE: My thirty minutes allotted for Coffee Date With
Random Internet Stranger are over. Well…Gonzo.
Thanks for sticking around.

JOHN: Thanks for returning my wallet.

(JADE sticks her hand out.)

JADE: Good meeting you, Gonzo.

JOHN: Good to meet you, Janice.

(JADE sits there.)

JOHN: I thought you had to go.

JADE: Yes, but I'm not leaving. This is where I work.

JOHN: I was going to work here, too. Look, I'll, uh, go
sit on the other side of the room.

JADE: No, don't worry about it. I'll move.

(JADE walks to the other side of the room where LOUISE and
TYLER sit. Lights go up on LOUISE and TYLER.)

(LOUISE and TYLER look at each other.)

TYLER: We've made it through every rough patch before. What makes this time different?

LOUISE: This time I decided to look at what's positive, instead of what I wish were different…

TYLER: Why? Why can't you look at what should be different? And try to fix it? …Like you did before.

LOUISE: What's positive is that I love you. And we've shared important things, children…and pain…and now I'm ready for my next adventure.

(JADE *looks up and observes.*)

TYLER: (*Starts to cry*) I'm not mad at you Louise. I'm just going to miss you so much. (*He continues to cry very loudly.*)

(LOUISE *notices* JADE *watching them.* JADE *immediately buries her head in her computer. Lights go down.*)

Scene 2

(*A screen appears on stage with the outlines of an iPhone or some sort of Smart Phone.*)

JOHN: happy hr?

JADE: Sure. What night?

JOHN: wrking 2nite :-(

JADE: Ok, let me know when.

JOHN: wed..wrk sux..

JADE: I think you wrote "Wednesday. Work Sucks." If that's true, OK. Please just give me a heads up.

JOHN: kogitacotruck…yum

JADE: ??

JOHN: innout…bleh

JADE: How are you?

JOHN: need vaca

JADE: Did you still want to have drinks on Wednesday? I'm available at 7.

JOHN: ah, srry lakers tix 2nite…mabe tmorw.

JADE: Didn't hear from you. Take it, no drinks.

JOHN: drnk w/ clients fckers. srry. :-(

JADE: Forget it. All of it.

JOHN: wtf?..chillout.

Scene 3

(One month later)

(Coffee Shop. JADE stands in line. She looks like she just rolled out of bed. The sounds of people talking, and grinding come out of the background.)

(LOUISE is sitting at a table working throughout this entire scene. She pays no attention to what is happening, but works on her computer.)

(JADE looks out into the audience, presumably out the door at someone outside. Her face registers recognition, surprise, curiosity.)

(JOHN suddenly walks in wearing shorts, running shoes, he looks like he's been sweating, and, yet, in a rush. He doesn't see JADE, and when he spots her, he turns to run out. Then he turns back. She tries to pretend she doesn't see him.)

JADE: I'll have an Iced Americano. *(Watches barista)* Three…make it four shots.

(JADE turns around and sees JOHN. She makes a dramatic, unconvincing gesture of surprise.)

JADE: Oh?! Hi John!

JOHN: Hi! *(To the barista)* I'll have two non-fat lattes.

JOHN: How are you?

JADE: *(At the same time)* How are you?

JOHN: *(At the same time)* Good.

JADE: Good.

(Dead silence)

JOHN: I can't chat too long.

JADE: *(Indicating outside)* I see.

JOHN: My friend is waiting.

JADE: Your "friend"?

JOHN: For lack of a better word. Look, I'm sorry...

JADE: No, I'm sorry. I have an antiquated need for direct communication. English. Full sentences.

JOHN: Work's been nuts...you know.

JADE: Look, John, just so you know, I prefer the blunt edges of honesty over the soft mushiness of fresh bullshit.

JOHN: Okay. Honestly, nothing personal, but I didn't want to hurt your feelings.

JADE: Okay. Honestly, nothing personal, but a whiffle ball would leave a greater imprint on my feelings.

JOHN: It's just...you know...

JADE: Relax. I'm just giving you a hard time. *(Nods outside)* I figured you'd find a more...more suitable situation. *(Motions to barista)* Is this an Americano? Thank you.

JOHN: *(To barista)* Two lattes? *(To JADE)* You make it sound so base. *(To barista)* Thank you. *(To JADE)* You know, you can learn a lot about someone by sleeping with them.

JADE: Like what to say to make them leave.

JOHN: That's the thing about you, Jade. You're very intense. You might want to scale back the attitude.

JADE: What attitude?

JOHN: The sharp spikes and points. I'd rather cozy up with a blanket of barbed wire.

JADE: Maybe I like to think of my "attitude" as a protective reef that wards off sharks, pirate ships and other unwanted situations.

JOHN: Like what?

JADE: Like being the chick standing outside of the coffee shop with a tied-up dog while the guy you're sleeping with talks to another woman.

JOHN: She's watching the bikes.

JADE: Well…what happened to your bike lock?

JOHN: I forgot the combination.

JADE: Did you try your birthday?

JOHN: Fine. Okay. So she's probably not "The One". But you can't expect to fall in love if you never go up to bat.

JADE: Well, you can't fall in love if you don't believe in the possibility of a love relationship.

JOHN: I believe in falling in love.

JADE: Just not with the person you're sleeping with.

JOHN: I'm not putting a gun to anyone's head.

JADE: No, just saying the right words that mold to a woman's particular brand of hopes and dreams.

JOHN: Is it my fault that women volunteer to sleep with me? They aren't my sex slaves.

JADE: No, but it's like immigrant labor; cheap because they feel they have no other choice. Nothing is free in this world. Except women.

JOHN: At least I'm not lonely.

JADE: Oh, you're lonely. You're way lonelier than I am. But instead of buffering myself with casual liaisons, I actually feel it.

JOHN: Look, you're right. I am being rude to my friend. Jade. Again, it's very interesting to talk to you. Not my idea of fun. See you around, if I'm unlucky.

(JOHN *walks.* JADE *watches for ten seconds. He returns.*)

JADE: Why do you carry so much cash?

(JADE *hands* JOHN *his wallet.*)

JOHN: You're a sociopath.

JADE: Sociopaths have no moral compass. I just want to finish what I had to say.

JOHN: (*Counts money*) You have thirty seconds…one… two. (*Silently continues to count*)

JADE: She entertained you. She gave you pleasure, helped you pass the time. You owe her more than a yeast infection and some poorly thought out line.

(*Puts wallet away*)

JOHN: Well, that's what she's getting.

JADE: Honesty. I dare say that's progress.

JOHN: You want honesty?

JADE: Yes, I want some fucking honesty.

JOHN: Fine. I don't want to lift a finger to get laid, and I don't have to. And, if it's that easy, so what? It doesn't matter, anyway. Because I won't see her after today. Because you know what I really want? The woman who is willing to do the most work and complain the least…

JADE: I have to apologize for robbing you blind…again, thereby wasting your, but mostly MY, precious time.

Good luck John with…your endeavors. *(She turns to leave.)*

JOHN: …Oh, and I forgot to add, the biggest honkers and the tightest…

JADE: You're an asshole!

JOHN: Is that from you or on behalf of the girl outside?

JADE: That's from me. *(Throws her coffee in his face)* That's for the girl outside.

(JOHN stands there, dumbstruck.)

(LOUISE looks up and takes notice. JADE notices her and then walks outside.)

Scene 4

(Coffee Shop. LOUISE sits with her computer. JADE walks in carrying her computer bag, she brushes past LOUISE. JADE wears jeans and a T-shirt.)

JADE: Excuse me, would this belong to you?

LOUISE: My Lord! That's my wallet! Where on earth did you find it..?!

JADE: It was in the restroom…

LOUISE: *(Opens wallet)* Well, somebody must have taken it because I didn't even use the rest room. *(Looks in wallet)* Well, that's strange, they didn't even take any money.

JADE: Probably some scared kid…is this seat taken?

LOUISE: No. I just got a few minutes to try to sync these things…I'm leaving in a minute, anyway.

(JADE sits down and pulls out her computer. While she talks, LOUISE appears to struggle with her phone and computer.)

JADE: You know, sometimes people take something not because they want it, but for the thrill of getting away with something. Of knowing something, of having a… secret. Then you have information, and, well, we live in the age of information.

LOUISE: *(Struggling with computer and phone)* Well, I can't blame anyone for stealing my wallet these days… *(Continues struggling, seems frustrated)* I don't understand how a regular person is supposed to…

JADE: Here let me…

(JADE *turns the computer around and, gently pulls the phone from* LOUISE. LOUISE *is slightly perplexed, but seemingly relieved as well.*)

LOUISE: My son used to do that for me…but he moved to the East Coast.

JADE: *(Working on* LOUISE'*s computer)* The ingrate. It's hard to imagine.

LOUISE: What is?

JADE: A grown man who once came out of my vagina. My only experience is of them coming in. *(Laughs like she said something funny)*

LOUISE: Do you have any children?

JADE: Just a brain child or two. And they seem to cause more trouble than their worth. I don't mean to be nosey, but…

LOUISE: Doctoral student. Biology. That's my thesis.

JADE: May I?

LOUISE: Better than my advisor. Go ahead.

JADE: "Female sand gobies who normally prefer more colorful males were found to be less choosy when exposed to a predator…"

LOUISE: I'm studying the mating strategies of Atlantic mollies, among other creatures...

JADE: Fascinating. *(Reads)* "...Females of the green swordtail usually prefer males with long swords." *(Looks up)* Wow, they really aren't that different from us mammals.

LOUISE: That's what makes them interesting.

JADE: *(Reads)* "However, they switch their preference towards males with short swords when exposed to videos showing successful predator attacks..."

LOUISE: The reasons for mate selection are far more varied and complicated than anyone has ever bothered to admit.

JADE: Well, the fear of predators might also explain the mating strategies of single, white biological-clock ticking professional women to spineless losers.

LOUISE: Not married?

JADE: I'm not exactly what you call "wife material." No, as soon as I make enough money, I'm going to hire one of my own.

LOUISE: A wife?

JADE: Yes, except I will call her an "assistant".

LOUISE: Well, if you don't want a child there is no mating strategy.

JADE: I never thought I wanted children...but my body...my body has a mind of it's own. Sometimes, I'll see a toddler and I could easily pick the kid up and run out the door.

LOUISE: Really?

JADE: *(Serious)* You have no idea. I've considered putting an ad out for a baby daddy...not just a sperm donor...someone with a high degree of shit-togetherness to raise the child.

LOUISE: Sounds like a lot to ask of someone you don't even know yet.

JADE: Even more to ask of me. I'm the one who's going to destroy my body.

LOUISE: What about falling in love?

JADE: Love. I've seen far greater women brought down by a homeless heroin addict who read too much Bukowski. I don't have that kind of time.

LOUISE: Yes. Speaking of which, I really should be going.

JADE: There is still one more update. It will only take one minute.

LOUISE: I see.

JADE: Tell me one thing...

LOUISE: And then will you give me back my computer?

JADE: Yes. Of course.

LOUISE: Go ahead.

JADE: If you hadn't married and had children, would you still feel that gaping hole in your soul?

LOUISE: Who said I had a gaping hole in my soul?

JADE: A figure of speech.

LOUISE: How'd you know that I was married?

JADE: I saw you here with a man, I believe he's your husband. He was crying. I'm sorry, I wasn't trying to eavesdrop, I swear.

LOUISE: He was never so vocal at couples counseling. (*Looks at* JADE) Can I have my computer back now?

JADE: Yes, of course. Just tell me one last thing.

LOUISE: Quickly.

JADE: Why are men so lost?

LOUISE: We're all lost.

JADE: I'm not lost.

LOUISE: Really?

JADE: I may still be at the crash site, but I'm not lost. The guys I meet, they don't even know they're on the island.

LOUISE: Well…

JADE: *(Extends hand)* Jade.

LOUISE: *(Shakes hand)* Louise. I don't know what to say.

JADE: Tell me to change conditioners, buy an eye serum, start shopping at the least condescending store between Forever 21 and Chico's.

(JADE hands LOUISE her computer. LOUISE packs it in her bag and gets up.)

LOUISE: *(Looks at computer, seems satisfied)* If that will make you feel better, go ahead. All I can tell you, Jade. There's nothing more strange than what goes on between two people "in love." That's why I study fish. Good-bye. And I like Chico's.

Scene 5

(Coffee Shop)

(Decor: Thanksgiving)

(JOHN sits at a table with DIRK [mid-40s], his boss and owner of the agency JOHN works at. DIRK possesses the magnetism of a man with a innate charisma, a lot of testosterone, and few moral scruples. He's intelligent in the way an animal is in the jungle. It seems like it takes effort for him to be human.)

DIRK: I want you at the meeting, sitting next to the client...

JOHN: You know I don't have anything to say at those things.

DIRK: All you need to say is, "It's going to look really fucking cool!"

JOHN: You know I hate saying that shit...I hate that word.

DIRK: Fucking?

JOHN: No, "Cool." Can't we use another word? ...Like, "dynamic", or "alluring"...

DIRK: What. The. Hell. Are we writing an essay for English class or talking about an ad for a video game?! Look, all they want to know is that you can reach a fifteen year-old who hasn't made eye contact in two years because his fingers are glued to his console.

JOHN: Don't you think the game's a bit violent?

DIRK: Are you fucking kidding me?!

JOHN: I just want to be able to sleep at night.

DIRK: Do you think I sleep at night? Man the fuck up. That's what happens when you don't have any responsibilities. You get soft, lazy, start wearing eighty dollar T-shirts, and jeans three sizes too small.

JOHN: I'm a creative director. If I didn't look artsy, the clients won't trust me.

DIRK: Look, get a pedicure, wear a black scarf, I don't give a shit. Just stop bitching about your job....

(JADE *enters. She's still wearing jeans but nicer shoes. She notices* JOHN, *and immediately turns to leave, pretending she didn't see him. She quickly looks back and notices him see her. She reluctantly walks over.*)

JADE: Hi.

(JOHN *tries to avoid looking at* JADE.)

JOHN: Hi.

JADE: *(To* DIRK*)* I'm sorry to interrupt.

JOHN: We're in a very important meeting.

JADE: *(To* JOHN*)* I wanted to apologize.

JOHN: Fine. Whatever. Forget about it.

JADE: Do you accept my apology?

(DIRK *stares at* JOHN.)

DIRK: *(To* JOHN*)* What'd she do?

JOHN: Nothing. Look, it's fine. *(To* JADE, *points to* DIRK*)* I'm busy.

DIRK: What's going on?

JADE: I threw a cup of iced coffee on him.

DIRK: *(To* JOHN*)* Did she really?

(JOHN *doesn't say anything.*)

DIRK: Awesome. *(To* JOHN*)* Don't be such a pussy. She apologized. Introduce us.

JOHN: Jade. Dirk. Dirk. Jade.

JADE: *(Extends hand)* I think we've met before.

JOHN: What?

DIRK: Oh, yeah. One of those networking things. Some fucking mobile/interactive/digital/we're-going-to-change-the-way-you-connect bullshit waste of time… been to a lot of those.

JADE: This one had cupcakes.

DIRK: Oh, yeah.

JADE: You were the one groaning loudly each time someone used the expression "engaging with the brand".

DIRK: I call it low level participation. Do you have a card?

JOHN: She's not…

JADE: It's probably not a good idea.

JOHN: Yes, trust me. She's not someone you want…

DIRK: *(Puts up hand to* JOHN*)* Stop talking. *(To* JADE*)* Call this number, talk to Tracy, set up a meeting for this afternoon.

*(*JADE *takes the number.)*

JADE: I think my rate just doubled.

DIRK: She's funny, too.

*(*JADE *walks away.* DIRK *smiles.)*

DIRK: Did you hit that?

JOHN: No…we went on one stupid coffee date. She's crazy. Insane. Psycho. Bi-otch with a capital B.

DIRK: *(Shakes his head)* You've got the same problem across the board. You can't pull the trigger.

JOHN: I didn't want to pull any triggers…!

DIRK: Where's the new business?

JOHN: I brought in the flower company

DIRK: Fucking plants? Old ladies. Where's the blood lust? Stop with the simpering. Just hit something. Anything! And move on.

JOHN: Look, she's not someone you want to work with. End of story. Let's just say, I'm not giving her a reference.

DIRK: Then don't hire her for the company you don't own.

JOHN: She steals. She lifted my wallet.

DIRK: They all do. *(Gets up)* Why else would we come back?

Scene 6

(Decor: Christmas/Holiday. Christmas tree in the corner)

(Lights go up on LOUISE sitting alone.)

(ROXANNE, [50s, White woman] enters the Coffee Shop. She stylishly stands at the counter talking to the barista. She takes up more space than the average customer.)

ROXANNE: Could I please see the soy container? *(She holds up soy container and reads before putting it back.)* I'm sorry, but it says that it's made from processed soy beans. Are you sure you don't have any almond milk? *(Listens for response)* Okay, then I'll take half non-fat milk and half soy, and just let the estrogen be what it is…and then don't add too much pumpkin spice flavoring…just half, but could the other half be mocha? Okay, and I want three shots. Great. You guys are the best. *(She looks around the room like she's surveying the scene, her eyes fall on LOUISE. She puts her hand on her heart like she's been deeply shocked. She approaches LOUISE.)*

ROXANNE: Louise. This isn't kosher, I know.

LOUISE: Roxanne! *(She stands as if to hug ROXANNE, but then shakes her hand)* It's great to see you.

ROXANNE: If this fortuitous chance bumping into each other, in a very different environment, brings up any feelings for you Louise, I completely understand.

LOUISE: No. I'm just…glad to see you. It's just like seeing a good friend.

ROXANNE: You look fantastic.

LOUISE: Thank you. Please. Sit down.

ROXANNE: Oh, I can't. I have an appointment. I just ran in for the pumpkin spice latte… *(She sits down.)*

ROXANNE: *(Serious, intense)* How are you?

LOUISE: I'm doing great. Tyler and I…

ROXANNE: *(Interrupts)* I figured. I know you struggled with that decision for a long time. I was there… remember?

LOUISE: You were. But you never put any pressure on me.

ROXANNE: No, I didn't. But whatever decision you made would have been fine with me.

LOUISE: We talk quite a bit. More than we did for some years of our marriage. I'm officially a doctoral candidate. I love my new place. I feel…free.

ROXANNE: Oh, I'm so happy for you.

LOUISE: I thought about maybe coming in again.

ROXANNE: Oh. That would be lovely. But that's impossible.

LOUISE: Why?

ROXANNE: I'm no longer practicing.

LOUISE: What? Why not?

ROXANNE: *(Gets up)* Time to change. Move on. I started focusing on the book I'm writing about sexuality and the Renaissance artists. And my practice lost it's pull on me…but you, Louise, hold a special place in my heart. Really. You do.

LOUISE: I could never have made these steps in my life without your support. I can't imagine that your service wouldn't be needed.

ROXANNE: Oh, Louise, that's very touching. But that was you. Not me.

LOUISE: Oh, that's not true.

ROXANNE: Analysis. It has it's pros and cons. I got to the point where I couldn't have a conversation without connecting the dots. I'm stuck with this Freudian free association bullshit. For instance, the song playing is "Summertime" from Porgy and Bess and see, strangely, I'm talking to a Black woman.... How fucking irritating is that?? ...It's like a cancer in my brain... If it hadn't been for Dr Chatsworth in grad school...I'm sorry, to talk your ear off.

LOUISE: No, it's very interesting.

ROXANNE: *(Starts to cry)* It's just been really hard....

LOUISE: Are you okay?

ROXANNE: ...since the suspension.

LOUISE: Suspension?

ROXANNE: ...a part of me really does miss seeing the inside of a person's soul. We live in this one dimensional world of cardboard cutouts...

LOUISE: Roxanne...what suspension?

ROXANNE: ...but it was all meant to be. I didn't really have the passion I once did. The drive to identify the relational dynamic, project it onto the screen of my relationship with the patient...my office, my church...and transform it into a thing of beauty. I just wanted the connection part, the feeling that I had gained a person's trust. A place where one word or compassionate look, could change a person's life. Like you. Did I help you?

LOUISE: Without a doubt.

ROXANNE: I did good work with you. Not to take too much credit. But look at you. You were a cowering mouse when you came to see me....

LOUISE: Roxanne. What happened?

ROXANNE: Jake came to see me. Twenty-two. Alive. Vivacious. His spirit, too big for this world. Then the board came in and started asking questions…and poor Jake's treatment was disrupted…

LOUISE: Why?

ROXANNE: Parents. These fucking helicopter parents, they don't understand The Process. Sexuality. Especially in a young male, is the identification with the infant state.

LOUISE: Roxanne…did you…?

ROXANNE: Feelings. They are powerful.

LOUISE: Roxanne. Did you sleep with your patient?

(ROXANNE *gets up.*)

ROXANNE: It's okay, Louise. It's better this way. It was so nice to see you. I'm not worried about you. Not at all.

(ROXANNE *extends her hand.* LOUISE *shakes it.*)

ROXANNE: Wonderful to see you.

LOUISE: Take care, Roxanne. And thank you for everything.

ROXANNE: My pleasure.

(ROXANNE *leaves.* LOUISE *sits alone for about five seconds. She picks up phone and dials.*)

LOUISE: Tyler…guess who I just…you know, never mind…sorry. (*Hangs up*)

(JOHN *enters. He looks around, sees* JADE *and slumps into the chair opposite her. She is focused on her computer, scarcely pays attention.*)

JOHN: I sat in that fucking Panda Express smelling office till midnight. Then the presentation got rescheduled. Then the client changed directions. And now we just killed the entire campaign. Hours of

work, beautiful, thoughtful work…fucking art! Gone.
Dead. I would rather kill baby kittens than go through
that nightmare again…okay, fine, baby mice…maybe
squirrels. I've always hated squirrels. *(Looks at* JADE)
What happened to you?

JADE: What do you mean?

JOHN: You look different. Did you change your hair?

JADE: I might have brushed it.

JOHN: Did you get a facial?

JADE: No. I've never gotten a facial in my life.

JOHN: It's good for your skin.

JADE: Do you get facials?

JOHN: Maybe. What? …I have really deep pores. *(Looks
at* JADE) You're glowing.

JADE: No. I'm not.

JOHN: Why are you blushing?

JADE: I'm not blushing.

JOHN: Did you have sex?

JADE: I don't have time to indulge your fantasy life
right now. I have work to do.

JOHN: You're sleeping with someone.

JADE: That's personal.

JOHN: Oh, so we're not personal anymore. I get it. Now
I get paid to listen to you.

JADE: No, I get paid to talk. You just have to listen to
keep your job.

JOHN: I don't believe it. You fucked my boss.

JADE: What?!

JOHN: I introduced you to him. You can at least be
straight with me about it.

JADE: I'm not sleeping with your douchebag boss.

JOHN: He's your boss, too.

JADE: No, he's my client.

JOHN: Why don't you just say, "He's my client…bitch!"

JADE: Fine… "He's my client, bitch?"

JOHN: Say it like you mean it.

JADE: Why?

JOHN: Because this is bullshit. I work my ass off for seven years only to sit next to a foosball table and a twenty-two year-old who thinks that the most exciting thing in the world is spending the night in the office. It used to seem important. Work was everything…. Now, if I hear that Radiohead album one more time I'm gonna off myself. There is other music…am I wrong?

JADE: I did sleep with someone. Not Dirk.

JOHN: I knew it. Vital statistics, please.

JADE: Name: Withheld. Age: twenty-five. Occupation: Rapper/Trader Joe's cashier.

JOHN: Rating?

JADE: Seven. That's all guys care about.

JOHN: Penis size?

JADE: Except that. John, it's not the size, it's the fit.

JOHN: A small penis and he still got a seven?! How did you meet?

JADE: He was passing out flyers to one of his shows. I had nothing better to do at eleven P M on a Tuesday night, so I went. I ended up dancing til three A M. So, I let him walk me to my car…I swear it's harder to find a taco stand than it is to get laid in L A.

JOHN: Final analysis.

JADE: Fun. I had fun.

JOHN: Morning after?

JADE: I wake up and I look at this hot young guy sitting next to me, and I think "What do I say to get him out of my apartment in the next five minutes?" I gave him a frozen waffle and made up some story about the plumber coming. Get this…I hope I never run into him again.

JOHN: Congratulations: now you're a dude.

JADE: Then that's terrible! It's sad.

JOHN: Trust me, he's not sad.

JADE: I don't understand men at all. Here you have a flesh and blood person, a human being, with dreams, and desires, and hopes and fears, someone's baby. And I don't give a shit about him. Of course I'm glowing. My body doesn't know that I've betrayed my soul.

JOHN: Your thinking about this is all wrong.

JADE: What if I'm becoming THAT woman?

JOHN: The one who would sleep with me?

JADE: Yes. That woman who has foregone all hope and faith in love.

JOHN: You're so extreme. Why is everything so black and white?

JADE: Is the sun out at night? Is there a dry spot at the bottom of the ocean? Are we alive or dead?

JOHN: Are you hungry?

JADE: I gotta finish this up… *(Pause)* Wait. Hold on. Stop. Are you asking me on a date?

JOHN: I just meant, as friends, colleagues, whatever.

JADE: Yes, well, friend, colleague, whatever…no, thank you.

JOHN: Why not?

JADE: Because I like the status quo. Talking to you within the confines of these four walls, muzak-like jazz, I can see the whole you. The dark side, the dude side.

JOHN: Do you really think you've seen my dark side?

JADE: A piece of it.

JOHN: That's funny. Sometimes, I don't think a girl means anything to me, until I've been a complete jerk to her at least once. It's like, if she doesn't know how big of a dick I can be, then she can't possibly really like me.

JADE: Well, then I'd hate to see you in love.

JOHN: I promise if you go out to dinner with me, I'll still be an asshole.

JADE: No, not now. I don't feel the line, yet.

JOHN: What line?

JADE: The line that excludes all possibilities.

JOHN: Why do you have to draw lines?

JADE: I don't draw them, they appear on their own by forces beyond my control. Haven't you just been interested in someone, and then you get to know them, and then the line appears and you realize you have no future in that relationship.

JOHN: No. That never happens to me. You know, Jade, there's only so much pontificating about relationships you can do. Eventually, you have to have one.

JADE: I've had relationships.

JOHN: When? In your twenties? Those weren't relationships, those were scenarios, workshops…what did you call them? Buffers against the loneliness?

JADE: You are hitting on me.

JOHN: Who cares?

JADE: I do. Because this isn't about me. It's about your sword fight with your douchebag boss. Why don't you take him to dinner?

JOHN: He likes to play hard to get.

JADE: And I thought you only liked cheap whores.

JOHN: Why are you easier to talk to than the women I date?

JADE: Because we share some common childhood pain.

JOHN: Yes, you're controlling and judgmental, just like my mother.

JADE: And you have the integrity of a pop rock, just like my father.

JOHN: I happen to think that pop rocks have a great deal of integrity. You know exactly what they're going to do.

JADE: They will explode in your mouth and ultimately give you cancer.

JOHN: I wasn't going to go there. Maybe I need four or five wives. Maybe I'm a polygamist.

(JADE starts to pack up.)

JADE: Maybe?! Or maybe you live relationship No Man's Land along with the rest of the terminally single. Your collection of nebulous attachments have become a shopping mall of needs. You have sex with this girl, talk to this woman, and confess your sins to…

JOHN: …you.

JADE: If that's the case, then you owe me a dinner.

JOHN: I can expense it.

JADE: No, I think you should pay.

(TYLER enters. He stops and stares at LOUISE.)

TYLER: What?

LOUISE: What are you doing here?

TYLER: I thought something happened to you.

LOUISE: Why?

TYLER: Because you called me. It was so good to hear from you. You look wonderful.

(LOUISE *throws a cup of water on him.* TYLER *just stands there stunned.*)

TYLER: What'd you do that for?

LOUISE: BECAUSE YOU LIED TO ME FOR TEN YEARS YOU FUCKING ASSHOLE!

(LOUISE *looks in her purse for some tissues and gives them to* TYLER.)

LOUISE: I'm sorry…I have to go… It's just water, it won't stain or anything. Good night. (*She leaves.*)

TYLER: (*Announces to the coffee shop*) It's all good. This is tremendous progress. I AM A HAPPY MAN.

Scene 7

(*Decor: Still Christmas*)

(*Coffee Shop.* DIRK *stands in line waiting for coffee, talking on his cell phone.* TYLER *walks in and stands beside him.*)

DIRK: Just tell him that I'll pick them up tomorrow… five hundred dollars! What? For fucking lacrosse gear?! …Look, I gotta run…. No, I'm working late…I'm in meeting…yes, with clients…yes, I'm with fucking clients! No, I won't be home till late…I don't know… really, really late! (*To barista*) …I'll have a double espresso shot…. (*To phone*) Bye! (*Hangs up*) Bitch.

DIRK: (*To* TYLER) Did you catch the score?

TYLER: Giants just hit a home run.

DIRK: Damn.

TYLER: I think it's over.

DIRK: They blew it.

TYLER: They had their chance.

DIRK: They sure did. You can't throw away opportunities.

TYLER: Well, if you do, you better be prepared to come back stronger than ever. More solid. You have to let it motivate you to rise above.

(JADE *walks in, acknowledges* DIRK *and takes a seat.*)

DIRK: *(Waves at* JADE*)* I say, always play against their weaknesses…because everyone's got 'em. *(Takes shot)* Take it easy.

(DIRK *sits down across from* JADE. TYLER *sits alone.*)

JADE: *(Glances at* TYLER*)* Male bonding.

DIRK: Doesn't take much. News, weather, sports. So, where's your skinny little art director friend?

JADE: I don't know. I figured he was slaving away for The Man. Or maybe got hit by a bus. Or bludgeoned by his pot dealer. Something violent, not swift.

DIRK: Fucking dirtbag. Remind me to kick his ass. Not even a text?

JADE: Not even a random non sequitur. "I'm hungry", or "Where's the nearest Yogurt Land?"

DIRK: Fucking yogurt… You gotta stay away from his type. They fuck you without telling you that they're fucking you. I say, if you're gonna fuck people, wear it on your shirt. Have it say "I'm going to fuck you". Then you have nothing to apologize for.

JADE: That's more information about your love life than I need.

DIRK: Now we both know that's not true.

JADE: Look, Dirk, generally speaking...I'm not that kind of slut.

DIRK: Then what kind of slut are you?

JADE: Organic. Fair trade. Drama free.

DIRK: So this is because I'm married?

JADE: And then there's your wife.

DIRK: Well, don't spend one minute worrying about that Marc Jacobs Bitch because she sure as hell isn't crying into the sands of Cabo while her diving instructor rubs sunscreen on her hairless hooch. But the douchebag...? Why do you care about that loser?

JADE: He's your darling. Maybe I don't want to suffer by comparison.

DIRK: Come on. You know he's not my type. I like them huskier, more pool hall trucker-like.

JADE: You admit it then, he's the wife that won't fuck you.

DIRK: Well, then that's one thing they have in common... Look, this is fun and all. But let's take it somewhere with better music, comfy chairs, and drinks the color of a Smurf. If I have to hear the sound of grinding beans for one more minute, I'm going to beat the crap out of one of those nerds.

JADE: No, I'd rather stay here. As I'm sure you know, there are plenty of women who find themselves helplessly attracted to married or attached men. But I prefer them single, and just plain emotionally unavailable.

DIRK: But that's what I am! Deep down inside. Clients don't trust single people. Wife. House. Kids. I needed the full set.

JADE: So that your clients will listen to you?

DIRK: My clients don't listen to me. They listen to white U S C frat boys who blast gangster rap from their Audis. I'm just the business man who hires that brand of asshole. *(Considers* JADE*)* You've never been married.

JADE: No. Of course not. I don't look good on a mantle.

DIRK: Ah, sure you do. You could find one of those nice, appreciative types. The kind that "value" their wives.

JADE: I don't meet those guys. Not until they're holding up arugula at the Farmer's Market and asking their wives, "Honey, will this go with the heirlooms?"

DIRK: No, that's not you. You like to hang at the deep end of the pool. Ideals. They'll fuck up your chances of being happy.

JADE: I don't have ideals.

DIRK: Oh, but you do.

JADE: Like what?

DIRK: Oh, like what's his face. He wants to create art. You. You want love.

JADE: I never said I wanted love…I mean…you know what I mean.

DIRK: Hon, love is all you want. If you didn't, you'd be strolling through Whole Foods looking for a bell pepper and ten types of olive oil for your husband's arugula fucking salad.

JADE: Or a nice Pinot. *(Pause)* What about your kids?

DIRK: What about them?

JADE: Do they ever factor into your decision making?

DIRK: There's Santa Claus, the Easter Bunny, and Dad. I bear gifts and hugs. They're cuter now that they're on meds. Look, I never said I was a great father. But I do love them.

JADE: You're just old school.

DIRK: Hey, watch the language…

JADE: You know what I mean. You pick up the check. And the phone. You dial. Even talk. Every girl feels special for five minutes.

DIRK: I hope longer than that.

JADE: It's all honey and sweetness from hello to good-bye.

DIRK: I hearken from a time when it was still hard to get laid.

JADE: I used to think guys like you were assholes. Now, I'm lucky to get a thank you. And if I do, it will be a text.

DIRK: Dudes want a challenge. If you're too easy, we regress to our infant state…. This. What we're doing.

JADE: Talking?

DIRK: Doesn't happen in my world. Look, if you wait around for the day when what's-his-face finally pulls his head out of his rectum, your boobs will look like a pair of socks filled with sand, and worse, your heart will crumble to the touch, like a cigar that's been left burning in the ashtray. I'm old enough to have seen it, and there's no going back. You're a beautiful woman. Netflix, cat, and a Cabernet? Or adoring Alpha male and steak? I don't see the choice.

JADE: They're putting up a good fight against gravity.

DIRK: What are?

JADE: My boobs.

DIRK: How do you like french food?

JADE: I'm more of a coffee and sushi girl.

DIRK: Fucking sushi. You could use a decent meal. Wine. Protein. Creme Brulee.

JADE: You know you could talk your way into Steve Job's grave.

DIRK: Yes. And I plan to.

Scene 8

(A few days later)

(Coffee Shop. DIRK stands at counter. He reaches into his back pocket, but realizes it's empty. He checks his pocket and jackets.)

DIRK: *(To barista)* Hang on, Hon. I can't find my wallet. Musta left it in my car.

(JOHN walks in and sits down.)

DIRK: I can't stay long.

JOHN: Sure. Hey, so I've been meeting with this small start-up networking site…it's like Twitter for dogs.

DIRK: You're fired, Dick Head.

JOHN: What?! Are you fucking kidding me?!

DIRK: Look, I'm doing you a favor, you pussy.

JOHN: I worked my ass off for you for seven years! How can you do this to me?

DIRK: You were supposed to steal my clients or get swiped by Chiat or some other fucking overrated frat house. That's what everyone else does. But no, you stay and whine about "the work". We don't make art. We're Client Services, we get fucked for a living.

JOHN: And I'm a little old to be pimped out.

DIRK: I'll give you a reference. I gotta go. My wallet's in the car.

(JOHN *gets up and stands close to* DIRK. *For a moment it seems like he's planning to hit* DIRK.)

DIRK: Are you fucking kidding?

JOHN: Go fuck yourself.

Scene 9

(JADE *enters wearing a black suit and heels. She looks noticeably professional, less casual. She seems like she's in a rush.*)

(LOUISE *is working…she is also dressed as if she's going somewhere important.*)

(JADE *notices* LOUISE *and stops.*)

JADE: Need help, Louise?

LOUISE: Oh, hello… Well. Yes…I don't want to bother you.

JADE: I need to feel useful. (*She sits down. She puts her stuff down and places a man's wallet on the table.*)

LOUISE: What's that?

JADE: It belongs to a friend. He left it at my house. (*Looks up*) I'm going to return it.

LOUISE: You find a lot of those.

JADE: Maybe they find me.

LOUISE: Well, then you must not be hard to find.

JADE: No, I'm not. I'm always here. But all that's about to change.

LOUISE: And why is that?

JADE: Because Louise, after you've been on the other side of passion enough times you know there's nothing there but a bunch of tumbleweeds and abandoned lots…

LOUISE: I've always loved tumbleweeds. They are free to go with the wind.

JADE: Well, then, maybe it's one long, empty hallway with no pictures and a part of you expects to see the twins from *The Shining*...whatever it is, hanging out there changes a woman. Either she gets lonelier or stronger, but either way she's less desperate to enter a room...and when she does it seems smaller and she takes up more space. And she notices things that she didn't notice before, like how she feels in it and whether or not she wants to leave.

(JADE *turns the computer back over to* LOUISE. *She stands up and picks up her stuff.*)

JADE: But the guys that she used to date...they haven't changed. They are all the same! Because they don't hang out in the boring Hallway of Nothingness... No, they just keep going from room, to room, to room... until all the rooms look the same...

LOUISE: Sometimes they remember the room they liked best.

JADE: No, Louise, you are wrong. We are all truly... alone. And that is why women have children. So WE can love something relevant. I get it now. Have a great day. *(She starts to leave.)*

LOUISE: Well, I love your outfit.

JADE: *(Turns around)* Just trying to look the part.

LOUISE: And what part is that?

JADE: A man.

Scene 10

(Decor: Still Holiday/Christmas. But it's close to January.)

*(*TYLER *sits beside* LOUISE. *On the table is a bouquet of flowers.)*

TYLER: I always said she was crazy.

LOUISE: You just didn't like her.

TYLER: She told you to leave me.

LOUISE: No, Tyler. She didn't tell me to do anything. She asked me what I thought and then I realized I didn't want a husband who lies to me.

TYLER: You're so beautiful.

LOUISE: Tyler, I'm being serious.

TYLER: I know. I'm listening. I'm just so in love with you.

LOUISE: Pleeze…

TYLER: I'm just saying it…I'm not expecting anything. Can a man not tell a woman he's in love with her? Have we become so cynical?

LOUISE: We're divorced.

TYLER: What's marriage got to do with it? With anything?

LOUISE: Can't you find someone younger? Hotter than me?

TYLER: Maybe. I don't know. I don't care.

LOUISE: Or is it the chase? Again. It never ends.

TYLER: Look, I don't even want to sleep with you. I just want to sit here and talk to you about that crazy bitch.

LOUISE: She's not crazy.

TYLER: Really?

LOUISE: She has needs. What's so wrong with sleeping with an attractive young man?

TYLER: He was her client. She might have hurt him more. Violated trust.

LOUISE: You violated my trust. I forgave you.

TYLER: Did you?

LOUISE: Not really.

TYLER: Well, then.

LOUISE: I'm a terrible judge of character.

TYLER: Maybe you just like human beings. That's not a fault.

LOUISE: I lived in a fantasy world about...us. There are no guarantees. Married. And we could be as estranged as two people passing through here. We're all just sharing a moment, or a thought, or...a child.

TYLER: Let's get a room.

LOUISE: Did you hear anything I just said?

TYLER: Not really. I'm just so attracted to you right now.

LOUISE: What the hell is wrong with you?

TYLER: I'm emotionally stunted, but madly in love with you. Are you in?

(JADE *walks in and sits at another table working. She nods at* LOUISE *and gets straight to work. She is dressed professionally, a suit and heels. Her hair is pulled back.*)

(JOHN *enters. He slumps in the chair across from her. He looks as if he's been on vacation. If this weren't a play he'd have a beard.*)

(JADE *looks up, notices him, and immediately turns back to her computer screen.*)

JOHN: Okay. So that's how it is. *(Pause)* Fine. I get it. *(Waits some more)*

(JOHN studies JADE for a moment, who is completely engaged in what she's typing. It's as if he's not there. He lets the moment hang till it's just too much.)

JOHN: I once read that Casanova was famous not for his seduction techniques, but the grace with which he extracted himself from his romantic liaisons.

(JADE glances at JOHN, looks back at her computer, continues to type.)

JOHN: I guess the Eighteenth Century was an easier time to be a man…ladies weren't all equal and shit… you could just relax and be yourself. Or maybe I'm just a pathetic excuse for a man….what do I do that's even remotely masculine? I create logos. If we all got wiped out by a flu virus, or a tsunami…would anyone need branding? No, we'd want firemen, paramedics, strong men with survival skills…I've never built a fire…I'm afraid of the barbecue…How many dudes do you know who hate to grill?

(JOHN seems to wait for some kind of reaction. JADE looks up momentarily and then goes back to her computer.)

JOHN: Look, I could tell you that it's a bad time for me. Or, that I met someone else. But you're not gonna buy any of that shit. A therapist once told me that I have problems with "intimacy" …whatever the fuck that is.

(JADE, finally, looks up. JOHN tries to read her for some kind of reaction.)

JOHN: I thought I was ready…for a minute there…I really did.

(JADE stares at JOHN.)

JOHN: So? You're mad… Not mad?

JADE: I'm busy, John.

JOHN: You're mad.

JADE: I'm not doing this.

JOHN: Doing what?

JADE: I'm not going to entertain you by losing my shit. You're free to sit there, but if you can't stay quiet, I'm going to have to find another table.

(JOHN *sits in silence.* JADE *continues to work.*)

LOUISE: See that girl sitting over there?

TYLER: Yes. I overheard her talking recently. Quite a character.

LOUISE: Well, one day, she comes over with my wallet. She found it in the bathroom. Then she sits down and she starts helping me with my computer. Then she starts talking up a storm…about relationships. I thought I'd never get out of there.

TYLER: Well, it looks like she found someone.

LOUISE: It certainly does.

(JADE *has been speaking to* JOHN, *but we don't hear it.*)

JOHN: What exactly do you mean by "I think you should go"?

JADE: I think you said what you needed to say.

JOHN: What did I say?

JADE: Something about firemen and paramedics, and how you carry a man purse but aren't a metrosexual.

JOHN: I don't carry a man purse. It's a satchel.

JADE: Look I'm not interested in being part of your wannabe harem of pathetic women.

JOHN: Please leave my harem out of this.

JADE: Look, you don't want me…

JOHN: And do you want me?

JADE: The chemical hormones do, but I definitely do not.

JOHN: Why not?

JADE: Because you're a man-child with no moral compass.

JOHN: Besides that.

JADE: You're rejecting me and you want to know why I would reject you….

JOHN: This is good. It's, uh, what do you call it? Debrief? Post-mortem?

JADE: Closure.

JOHN: Fine. Honestly, I don't think you could ever accept me for who I am.

JADE: You are correct in that assumption.

JOHN: Your turn.

JADE: Really?

JOHN: I'm giving you the floor. You don't want me because…

JADE: …Because…because what I really want deep down inside can't be had by 24/7 togetherness, or public vows, or shared bank accounts or children, or the fulfillment of sexual fantasies, and sentimental cards. What I really want is not something most women, after a certain point, even try for because they think it's utterly hopeless. It's free and takes only a flicker of a second…

JOHN: You're never going to meet that guy.

JADE: If I spend the next forty years of my life trying then that's an old lady I'd like to have a glass of wine with.

(JOHN *stands up. He checks his pants and his shirt.*)

JADE: I've retired from my life of crime.

JOHN: Why?

JADE: It's too easy. You put the X in the middle box and you've already won the game.

JOHN: Good-bye Janice73.

JADE: Have a nice life, Gonzo.

(Just as JOHN is about to walk out the door, he stops and stares out, as if he's seen something surprising.)

(DIRK walks in.)

JOHN: What are you doing here?

DIRK: Getting coffee. What the fuck do you care?

JOHN: What's going on here?

DIRK: I'm meeting Jade….

JOHN: Why?

DIRK: Is something the matter?

JOHN: I don't believe it. You piece of dog shit!

(JOHN suddenly grabs DIRK by the collar and pushes him against the wall. Everyone stares.)

JOHN: Every creative thought. Fine. The whole female account team?! Okay. My copywriter…whatever… but for God's sake…but seriously, is nothing sacred to you?!

DIRK: Don't be stupid, John. I will ruin you.

JOHN: You're an animal.

DIRK: On second thought, I'll still give you a reference…

(DIRK peels JOHN's arm and grabs him by the collar in one physical motion. He throws him up against the wall. He then looks around, as if he's suddenly realized that he's in a public place. Like a lion picking up a cub, he pulls JOHN outside.)

DIRK: …but I will kick your ass.

(LOUISE *and* TYLER, *suddenly get up and walk to the fourth wall, the window out to the parking lot, while* JADE *sits there transfixed.*)

(LOUISE *and* TYLER *suddenly grimace, as* JOHN *is clearly getting his ass kicked.*)

LOUISE/TYLER: Oh! Ouch!

LOUISE: I can't watch anymore.

LOUISE: *(To* JADE*)* Should I get someone?

JADE: Best to let nature take it's course.

TYLER: I have never seen white men in such an excited state.

JADE: The parking attendant is coming.

TYLER: He looks like he's never hit anyone in his life…. oh!

LOUISE: Tyler, do something.

TYLER: Why?

LOUISE: Tyler!

(TYLER *goes outside.* JADE *and* LOUISE *look outside throughout the following dialogue.*)

JADE: Louise…tell me something. How does a woman ever have faith in love…after a lifetime of disappointments?

LOUISE: Selective memory.

JADE: What about the Atlantic mollies?

LOUISE: They're the lucky ones.

JADE: Can't we just be done?

LOUISE: I think I'm in love with my ex-husband.

JADE: I suppose yours is the way of the living.

(LOUISE *sits down beside* JADE *and gently pats her shoulder.*)

(JADE *and* LOUISE *are transfixed and silent. Something has changed in the action going on outside.*)

JADE: What is he saying?

LOUISE: How would I know? I hardly understand what he says to me.

(TYLER *walks back in practically carrying* JOHN. JOHN's *nose is bleeding and his shirt is ripped and covered in blood and dirt. His hair is a mess. He clearly has gotten his ass kicked.* TYLER *seats* JOHN *back down next to* JADE.)

TYLER: Come on Louise, let's go.

LOUISE: I don't think I can hang out here anymore. Too much excitement for me.

(JOHN *looks close to death.*)

JOHN: Jade…I don't know what you call it…I know you don't like the words "marriage", or "wife", or "girlfriend", but, if you can think of a word for the person you try to talk to everyday, then I need to become that person in your life.

(JADE *is quiet.*)

JOHN: Say something.

(JOHN *puts his head between his hands and slumps down.*)

JADE: I'm pregnant.

(Lights out.)

END OF PLAY

AFTERWORD

I began writing this play shortly after the recession, in 2010, while unemployed and single. I spent every day in a coffee shop where I struggled to write a book. I wrote the play at first as a sketch for my own relief and amusement. And then it broke through me like a dam. Unlike the book, I looked forward to writing the play every day, like a favorite T V show or an old friend. It was something to come home to. I had no expectations, just the idea of men and women as utterly alien to each other and forced together in a small consistent space, like the coffee shop I sat in. When I was done I sent it to my friend, Joe Keyes, who suggested that I host a reading. One night, a dozen friends piled into my apartment to read a three hour draft about dating in Los Angeles. Only two people fell asleep.

More rewrites, apartment readings and staged readings followed until multiple people encouraged me to produce it. Everything that came after emerged from it's own momentum. Even the suggestion by my friend Cicely to remount it because our culture had shifted enough to make it more timely in 2019 than it had been in 2014. Our culture will probably shift again and again, and who knows if this piece will stay relevant, considering its focus on heterosexual relationships and women helplessly drawn to men. However, while society's acceptance of fluid genders and orientations has improved, I can't imagine that respect for women's bodies will reach a satisfactory place (certainly not in the world at large) or that sex will ever stop confounding humanity.

I thank my mother who drove me to countless theater classes, auditions and stood behind every creative idea. Ironically, the real heartbreak of my life was not caused by a romantic relationship with the man, but her passing. I wish she were here to see this publication. But that story is another play.

Thank you to everyone who came to readings and performances and supported the process. I hope it continues to be as fun to read, watch or perform as it was to write.

www.ingramcontent.com/pod-product-compliance
Lightning Source LLC
Chambersburg PA
CBHW070030110426
42741CB00035B/2705